State Facts for Fun!

Alaska

By Wyatt Michaels

Image courtesy of Images of Money

What was the purchase price per acre when Alaska was bought from Russia?

- A. $1 per acre
- B. $.10 per acre
- C. $.02 per acre

Image courtesy of yatoobin

The answer is C. Two cents per acre

On March 30, 1867, Secretary of State William H. Seward agreed to purchase Alaska from Russia for $7.2 million. That would be about $119 million in today's dollars for almost 600,000 square miles of land.

Image courtesy of discgolfer1138

What breed is the Alaska state dog?

A. Alaskan Husky
B. Alaskan Malamute
C. Siberian Husky

Image courtesy of JSF539

The answer is B. Alaskan malamute

It recently became the state dog in 2010. The breed has contributed greatly to Alaska's history and is still actively used today.

Image courtesy of cubby_t_bear

What city is the capital of Alaska?

A. Anchorage
B. Fairbanks
C. Juneau

Image courtesy of mathplourde

The answer is C. Juneau

It is the only capital not connected by road to the rest of the U.S. highway system. It became the capital in 1906.

Image courtesy of public domain

What is cheaper to buy in Alaska than in the "lower 48"?

- A. Gas
- B. Heavy coats
- C. Seafood

Image courtesy of Robert S. Donovan

The answer is C. Seafood

The abundance of seafood in many
different locations keeps the cost down
while gas prices usually run at least 30
cents higher than the national average
because of weather and transportation
challenges.

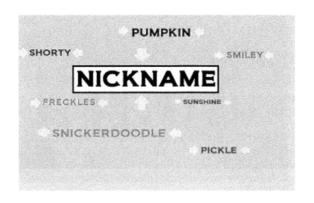

Image courtesy of Kalyn Lorenz

What is the nickname for Alaska?

A. The Last Frontier
B. Wilderness Majesty
C. Gold Peaks

Image courtesy of Alaskan Dude

The answer is A. The Last Frontier

It is also known as Land of the Midnight Sun and Seward's Icebox.

Image courtesy of 401(K) 2013

What is one of Alaska's main industries?

A. Tourism
B. Lumber
C. Oil and gas

Image courtesy of toffehoff

The answer is C. Oil and gas

Since 1977 the Alaska Pipeline has transported about 17 billion barrels of oil from Prudhoe Bay to waiting ships at Valdez Marine Terminal.

Image courtesy of A Train

Which national park is located in Alaska?

A. North Cascades
B. Katmai
C. Great Basin

Image courtesy of Marshmallow

The answer is B. Katmai

Alaska has eight national parks. Katmai is where over 2000 brown bears come each year to catch salmon. North Cascades Park is in Washington, and the Great Basin Park is in Nevada.

Image courtesy of dianecordell

When did Alaska become a state?

- A. 1959
- B. 1905
- C. 1867

Image courtesy of snowpeak

The answer is A. 1959

It became the 49th state on January 3, 1959.

Image courtesy of public domain

How far is it from Russia to Alaska?

A. 90 miles
B. 20 miles
C. 3 miles

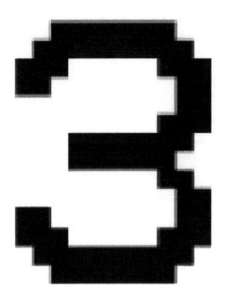

Image courtesy of striatic

The answer is C. 3 miles

The Russian Big Diomede Island is 3 miles from the Alaskan Little Diomede Island.

Image courtesy of eleephotography

Which large body of water does not border Alaska?

A. Pacific Ocean
B. Yukon River
C. Arctic Ocean
D. None of the above

Image courtesy of Gareth Sloan

The answer is B. Yukon River

Over 2000 miles long, the Yukon River is in the state of Alaska but not significantly on its border. Besides the Pacific and Arctic Oceans, Alaska is also bordered by the Bering Sea/Strait, the Chukchi Sea, and the Gulf of Alaska.

Image courtesy of jontintinjordan and woodleywonderworks

What is the difference between the highest and lowest temperatures recorded in Alaska?

A. 60 degrees
B. 100 degrees
C. 180 degrees

Image courtesy of jontintinjordan

The answer is C. 180 degrees

The highest temperature is 100 degrees in 1915, and the lowest temperature is -80 degrees in 1971.

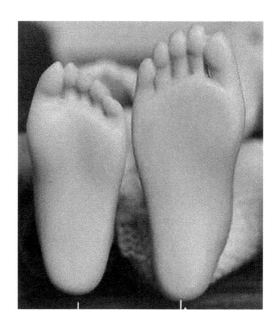

Image courtesy of ResinMuse

What is Alaska's rank in size?

A. First
B. Second
C. Third

Image courtesy of Ruby W.

The answer is A. First

It is more than twice the size of Texas that ranks second.

Image courtesy of Fredlyfish4

What is the name of the highest mountain peak in Alaska?

A. Mt. McKinley
B. Mt. St. Elias
C. Mt. Blackburn

The answer is A. Mt. McKinley

Rising over 20,000 feet, Mt. McKinley is the highest mountain in Alaska as well as all of the United States. Over half of the 20 tallest peaks in America are in Alaska.

Image courtesy of public domain

What is Alaska's state motto?

    A. Land of Liquid Gold
    B. North to the Future
    C. Seward's Folly

Image courtesy of woody1778a

The answer is B. North to the Future

The motto was adopted in 1967, during the 100 year anniversary celebration of the purchase of Alaska.

Image courtesy of North Charleston

Which state is neighbor to Alaska's border?

A. Washington
B. Idaho
C. Montana
D. None of the above

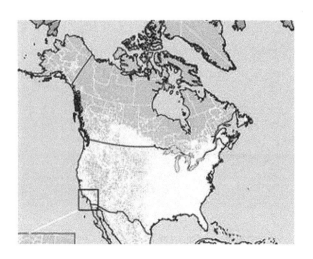

Image courtesy of SEDACMaps

The answer is D. None of the above

About 500 miles of Canada separate Alaska from Washington.

Image courtesy of Rennett Stowe

What is officially Alaska's state sport?

A. Dog Mushing
B. Hockey
C. Snow skiing

Image courtesy of Alaskan Dude

The answer is A. Dog mushing

It was adopted as the state sport in 1972.

Image courtesy of jimmywayne

What symbol is on the Alaska state flag?

A. Bear
B. Salmon
C. Stars

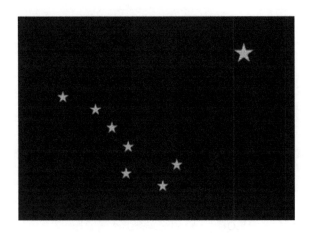

Image courtesy of public domain

The answer is C. Stars

Bennie Benson was 13 years old when he designed the flag in 1926.

Image courtesy of Lee Edwin Coursey

What has more coastline than Alaska?

    A. Florida
    B. Maine
    C. California
    D. None of the above

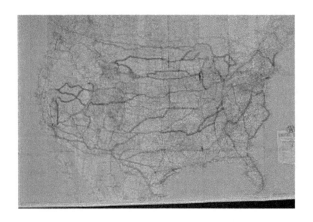

Image courtesy of El Cajon yacht club

The answer is D. None of the above

With more than 6600 miles Alaska has more coastline than all the other states combined.

Image courtesy of Dèsirèe Tonus

What is Alaska's state bird?

A. Willow Ptarmigan
B. Pacific Loon
C. Mosquito

Image courtesy of DenaliNPS

The answer is A. Willow Ptarmigan

Willow Ptarmigans turn completely white in the winter. Sometimes the mosquito is jokingly referred to as the state bird.

Image courtesy of leoplus

Alaska is in which time zone?

A. Pacific
B. Asian
C. Aleutian

Image courtesy of kla4067

The answer is C. Aleutian

Part of Alaska is also in the Alaskan time zone.

Image courtesy of Jeff Pang

How many lakes does Alaska have?

A. 1,000
B. 50,000
C. More than 3 million
D. None of the above

The answer is C. More than 3 million

Alaska has more than 40% of the surface water in the U.S. "Only" about 3,000 of the lakes are named. Lake Iliamna in southwest Alaska is America's second largest fresh water lake.

Image courtesy of Guzmán Lozano

Which city in Alaska is the most populated?

A. Anchorage
B. Ketchikan
C. Nome
D. Fairbanks

Image courtesy of Barrett Discovery

The answer is A. Anchorage

With almost 300,000 people, Anchorage has almost half of Alaska's population.

Image courtesy of D-Stanley

What is the name of the longest tunnel in Alaska?

A. Eisenhower
B. Anton Anderson
C. Hanging Lake

Image courtesy of NAParish

The answer is B. Anton Anderson

At 2.5 miles long, it was the longest tunnel in the U.S. until recently. It is for cars and trains! Eisenhower tunnel in Colorado is the longest high mountain tunnel.

Image courtesy of Lola's Big Adventure!

What is Alaska's state flower?

A. Delphinium
B. Forget-me-not
C. Peony

Image courtesy of pixelshoot

The answer is B. Forget-me-not

The colors of the Alaska flag match the colors of its state flower.

Image courtesy of Snap®

What famous sporting event takes place in Alaska every year?

- A. Island Tag Race
- B. Anchorage Air Race
- C. Iditarod Trail Sled Dog Race

Image courtesy of Arthur Chapman

The answer is C. Iditarod Trail Sled Dog Race

The race covers over 1100 miles from Anchorage to Nome. In 1985, Libby Riddles, the first woman to win the race, completed the race in 18 days, 2 minutes, 17 seconds.

The record set in 2014 was just over 8 days and 13 minutes.

Image courtesy of Capt' Gorgeous

Alaska ranks first in size, but where does it rank in population?

A. 47th

B. 48th

C. 49th

The answer is A. 47th

In 2010, it ranked above Vermont, North Dakota, and Wyoming.

Image courtesy of zieak

How long is the Trans-Alaska Pipeline?

A. 1,520 miles
B. 800 miles
C. 375 miles
D. None of the above

The answer is B. 800 miles

The Pipeline can transport more than 2.1 million barrels of crude oil per day. Heat pipes in the column mounts disperse heat upwards and prevent melting of permafrost.

Image courtesy of logatfer

What is Alaska's state tree?

A. Norway Maple
B. Western Hemlock
C. Sitka Spruce

Image courtesy of 5u5

The answer is C. Sitka Spruce

Sitka Spruce trees are the tallest conifers in the world. The Sitka Spruce became the official state tree in 1962.

Image courtesy of Colin K

Alaska is the _____ state in the U.S.

    A. Northernmost

    B. Westernmost

    C. Easternmost

    D. All of the above

Image courtesy of Alan Klim

The answer is D. All of the above

Part of Alaska is east of the International Date Line (though they moved the line to keep Alaska all in the same day) making it the easternmost as well as the westernmost and northernmost state.

Congratulations! You did it! You are now an expert on the state of Alaska.

Look for more quiz books by Wyatt Michaels about dog breeds, baseball, farm animals, careers, football, horses, presidents, other states, and more.

Lightning Source UK Ltd.
Milton Keynes UK
UKHW020701270620
365588UK00006B/136